EYNSHAM OXFORDSHIRE

A VILLAGE AND ITS ABBEY..

Eynsham is a village situated six miles west of Oxford in the Upper Thames Valley. Supporting a population of around 5000 people, it retains most of its medieval core, and a strong community identity. Between 1989 and 1992 Oxford Archaeology excavated a large part of St Peter's churchyard in Eynsham, in advance of graveyard expansion. They not only found the remains of the great Benedictine abbey that had dominated the village for over 500 years, but also important clues to the earlier history of both the site itself and the earliest human settlement at Eynsham. Blending the information from the dig with historical documents, this book charts the evolution of the village and the sacred site at its heart.

What do the symbols mean?

This symbol highlights sections of text that deal with the results of the 1989-1992 excavations.

Sections preceded by this symbol explain in more detail parts of Eynsham's story.

IN THE BEGINNING

PREHISTORIC EYNSHAM

Eynsham as a village did not exist until well after the Romans had come and gone, but the place was important long before. In only a few places along its length could the Thames be crossed without a bridge. At this point, which one day would become a ferry and later still Swinford Bridge, the river was shallow enough to wade across, and the site of the later abbey was the first high ground on the west side, at a possible crossroads of two important routes.

The dig found a deep ditch - called an enclosure. Pieces of pottery from the ditch show that it was dug over 3000 years ago. Nearby were a number of deep pits and the site of a circular building. What were they for? The ditch could have been a defence, with the earth dug out of the ditch used to make a bank alongside. Was this to keep animals inside, or intruders out? We cannot know. But there is another possibility - maybe the site had a sacred purpose. A large weathered stone was found in the ditch – it could have been a standing stone, like those at Rollright, near Chipping Norton. It's not something we can ever prove or disprove, but it might mean that the site of the abbey was important to people long before Christianity came to the land.

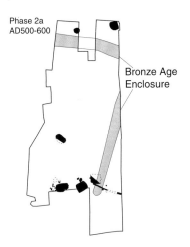

Phase 2a
AD500-600

Bronze Age
Enclosure

Above: The excavated weathered sarsen that may have stood as a single route marker or as part of a religious monument.

The Romans in Eynsham?
A number of Roman coins and some pieces of tile were found in the dig, but no building remains. This could mean that the modern churchyard area was farmland in the Roman period, but at least one building - possibly even a small villa - may have stood nearby, probably close to the road leading up from the river and heading west. Traces of a small settlement, possibly a farm, were also found in the region of the later abbey fishponds.
The nearest large Roman settlements to Eynsham were the small towns of Alchester (near Bicester), and Dorchester.
Most of the large villas, like North Leigh and Shakenoak, were situated in the Cotswolds.

The enclosure at Eynsham 3000 years ago.
It may have stood close by a junction of
rough tracks leading up from the river,
and going west and north.

OUT OF THE DARKNESS

SAXON EYNSHAM

The first mention of Eynsham is as the spoils of war. The Anglo-Saxon Chronicle states that, in the year 571 AD, 'Cuthwulf fought against the Britons at Biedcanford, and captured four vills - Limbury, Aylesbury, Benson and Eynsham (Egonesham); and in the same year he died.' Cuthwulf was a King of the West Saxons - the Gewisse. Even if we still do not know exactly why, this entry in the Chronicle must mean that Eynsham was an important place, perhaps the centre of a large estate.

Who were the Gewisse ? The history of the region after the Roman period is still murky, and what is known comes largely from objects found in burials. The Upper Thames seems to have been an area settled by different groups of Saxon settlers from modern day north-west Germany. Through the sixth century AD these groups merged into one, known in old chronicles as the 'Gewisse' - which in Old English means 'trusties' - or 'people who could be trusted'. To their west were the Hwicce, from whom "Wychwood" is derived. To the north were the Middle Angles. Communities were often centred on still-visible prehistoric earthworks like barrows or large enclosures like the one revealed in the dig, but they would still be very spread out, so it is difficult to tell where a community began and ended. Slowly these communities would be collected together in large estates, under the control of local chieftains.

What are the Anglo-Saxon Chronicles? This is a history written by the Saxons in the 8th and 9th centuries about their ancestors in England. It was based on oral traditions handed down from generation to generation, so the exact dates of events may not be reliable, but it still gives a good idea of the way the Saxon settlers became a nation

The Upper Thames region in Saxon times.

● Places recorded in Anglo-Saxon Chronicles   ——— Rivers

Wilsaete   Anglo saxon tribal territories   -·-·-·- Oxfordshire border

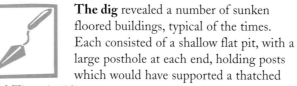

The dig revealed a number of sunken floored buildings, typical of the times. Each consisted of a shallow flat pit, with a large posthole at each end, holding posts which would have supported a thatched roof. These buildings were quite small and may have been used as workshops or weaving sheds, rather than houses to live in. Each building would last for maybe twenty years or so, and the pit would be used for rubbish once the building was abandoned. Among this rubbish was found pottery typical of the time, black in colour, sometimes with stamped decoration around the sides.

Left: One of the sunken floored Saxon buildings found in the course of the excavations.

Below: How two of the sunken floored buildings may have looked.

Below: Typical Saxon pottery of the 6th century (found in Abingdon).

The coming of Christianity

In about 820 AD the estate of Eynsham, with its minster (church), was part of the settlement of a bitter argument between King Coenwulf of Mercia and Archbishop Wulfred of Canterbury. The importance of the estate is indicated by its size - 300 hides.

Most of the conversion of England to Christianity took place in the 7th century AD. Some of the impulse to change came from monks like Augustine, sent from Rome, but other influences were the early church in Northumbria and from the opposite direction, the surviving Celtic church in Ireland. Yet pagan beliefs and symbols survived, just below the surface.

All these influences showed at Eynsham in the finds from the dig, including an Irish buckle, a Northumbrian styca (coin), and a stirrup-mount with a Viking-style decoration.

The plaster wall as it was uncovered.

 The dig produced evidence of timber and plaster buildings, with carefully sawn wooden uprights and limewashed plaster. These buildings seemed to form an organised group set within little paddocks. The church, which also was wooden to start with, probably stood to the north of the dig. A group of priests or canons would have lived here, taking services in the church.

A buckle with Irish decoration.

What is a hide?

A 'hide' was a measure of land area in Saxon and medieval times. It represented that amount of land sufficient to support a single family, and was calculated in terms of how much tax it would produce, and so could measure different sizes depending on how good the land was. This is one year's tax demand from ten hides in the 8th century:

"ten vats of honey, 300 loaves, twelve ambers of Welsh ale, thirty of clear ale, two full grown cows or ten wethers, ten geese, twenty hens, ten cheeses, an amber full of butter, five salmon, twenty pounds of fodder and 100 eels"

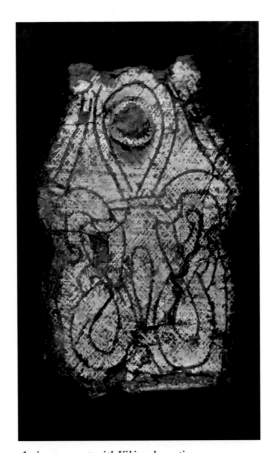

A stirrup mount with Viking decoration.

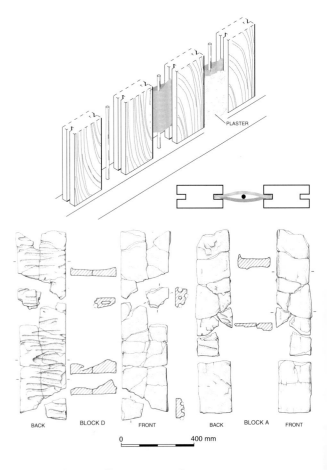

How the plaster wall was constructed.

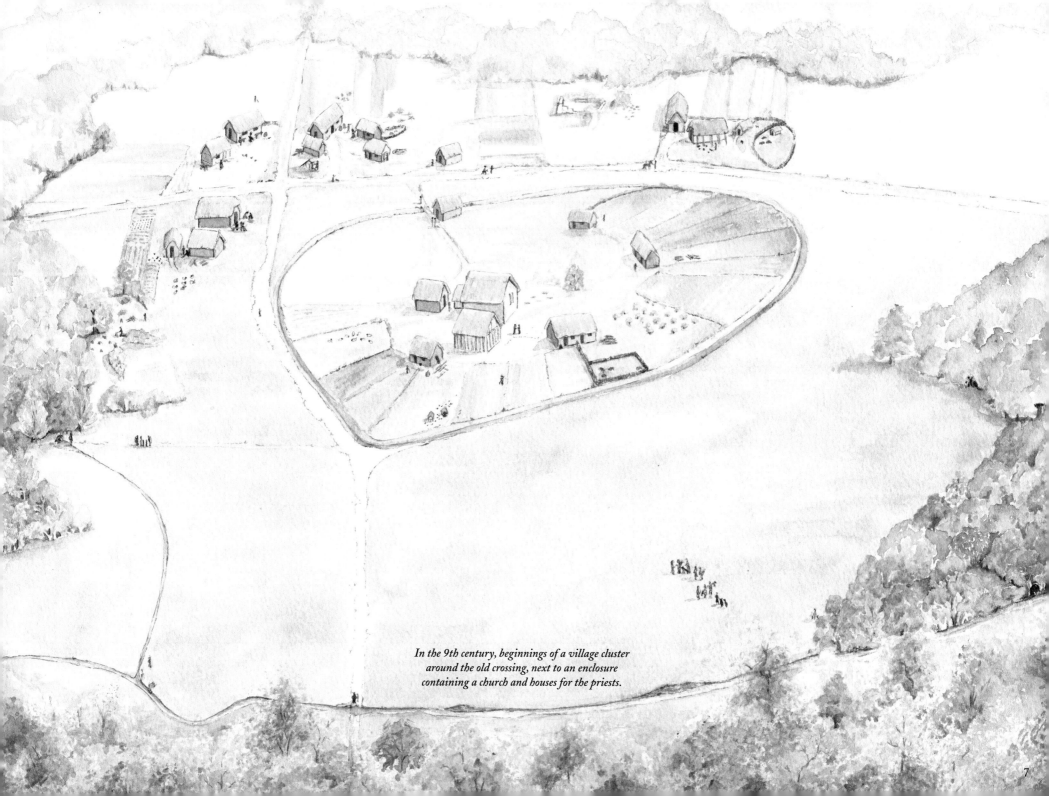

In the 9th century, beginnings of a village cluster around the old crossing, next to an enclosure containing a church and houses for the priests.

Foundation 1005

The early 11th century was a dangerous time, with fresh waves of Viking attacks across the North Sea. The doing of good works in God's name, like the foundation of a new monastery, would be like a sacrifice, ensuring God's help in resisting the invaders.

In 1005 the charter founding the abbey began with these words:

> Aethelred "by the grace and mercy of God, king and ruler of the realm of the English gives authority to Aethelmaer, a man of outstanding loyalty to myself and very dear to me" to establish a monastery 'at an important place, hard by the river Thames, and called Eynsham by those who live in that part of the country" ("in loco celebri juxta fluvium qui vocatur Tamis constituto, quod ab incolis regionis illius Egnesham nuncapatur vocabulo")

To provide material support for the new abbey, Aethelmaer donated several lands and manors - some close by like Shipton-on-Cherwell and Yarnton, some far afield like Thames Ditton in Surrey and Rameslie in Sussex.

The boundaries of the abbey estate around Eynsham were described very precisely:

> "these are the boundaries of the land at Egnesham. First from the 'rough lake' to Bugga's Brook; along the brook to Tilgar's ditch; from the ditch to ward sty [i.e. path]; from the sty to Winburh's 'stock'; from the stock to three oaks; along the way to the boundary tree; thence along the way to the port street; from the street to the 'swains' croft; thence to heath-field to the old ditch; thence right to the boundary-brook; along the brook into [the] Bladen; along [the] Bladen into [the] Thames".

Aethelmaer

In the late 10th century, England was ruled by Aethelred (the Unready), supported by a group of nobles, called eaorldermen, each of whom had authority over a number of large estates. Aethelmaer the Fat was eaorlderman of the western provinces, and he owned the estate with Eynsham at its heart.

Aethelred (the Unready) King of England 979-1016.

Aelfric

Aelfric was born around the middle of the 10th century AD and became a monk at Winchester, later moving to the abbey of Cernel (Cerne Abbas, Dorset). There he remained until 1005, when took up the office of abbot at Eynsham, offered by his good friend Aethelmaer. While at Cernel, he composed many of his best known writings, and his main strength was in taking obscure and difficult Latin texts and making them understandable to ordinary monks, who would not usually be very well educated.

Aelfric was well aware of the dangerous times in the late 10th century. One of his works begins:

> "I attempted this work .....because people especially need good teaching at this time, which is the ending of the world."

Soon after Eynsham Abbey was founded, Aelfric wrote his 'Letter to the Monks of Eynsham' in which he detailed the way the monks should conduct themselves from day to day.

We do not know precisely when Aelfric died - it was probably around the year 1010 - but it is likely that he was buried at the abbey, possibly in front of the church altar. The dig did not reveal Aelfric's church, so his body may lie there still.

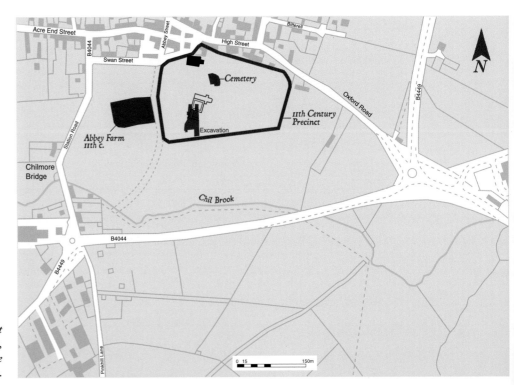

The possible layout of the first abbey, in relation to the modern village.

Building Aelfric's abbey

The construction of an abbey was a huge undertaking, needing skilled workers from far afield, or even abroad. Masons, glaziers, carpenters, roofers, along with labourers of all descriptions would swarm over the wooden scaffolding, as the buildings slowly took shape. There was no architect - a master mason would be in charge, and he would work with no plans, only sketches drawn on a dirt floor, and the experience of previous work.

All of the stone building required a lot of mortar. The dig found two bases of mortar mixers. Each would have been a shallow pit, with a large central post supporting a long wooden beam, with paddles hanging down. Labourers would turn the beam, and mix the mortar. Alongside the mortar mixers were puddles of mortar, where it was spilled as it was carried to the masons at work!

Enough of Aelfric's abbey was uncovered to show that it was probably one of the first in this country to be laid out with a cloister, and even pieces of the thick mortar floor of the cloister, where Aelfric himself would have walked, were recovered.

How the building site may have looked.

Did Aelfric himself walk on this floor?

The two mortar mixers.

Life in God's house

The principal part of a monk's day was taken up with prayer. Benedictine monks prayed together seven times a day, including once in the dead of night and again at daybreak.

The manual work included tending gardens, overseeing the business of the monastery, and various housekeeping and maintenance chores. In addition, monks began to take on other activities, the most important of which was the copying of books.

Other monks who were skilled with their hands produced decorated book covers or ivory carvings.

 The dig found two beautiful pieces of carved ivory - one a part of a casket lid, made of elephant ivory, the other, in walrus ivory, was a tiny figure of St John.

Unfinished figure of St John made of walrus ivory.

Fragment of a casket lid, made of elephant ivory.

The reliquary of St Benedict.

A gift to the village

What is now St Leonard's Church began life as the north gate of Aelfric's abbey, and possibly of the minster church before it. Later a chapel was built at the gate. As the village grew, the monks found it difficult to hold their services in a church also used by the people, so they gave the chapel to the village, and kept the abbey church for themselves.

 What was the Benedictine Rule?

With the spread of Christianity into western Europe, many early monasteries were established, but each followed their own rules. Benedict, the abbot of Monte Cassino in Italy, was the first to write down, in 73 chapters, a complete book of rules for the correct running of a monastery, and the correct behaviour of a monk. The rule emphasised obedience, silence and humility, and stressed the importance of manual labour as well as prayer and worship.

After his death, his bones were recovered by his followers, and brought to lie in the church of St Benoit-sur-Loire, in France.

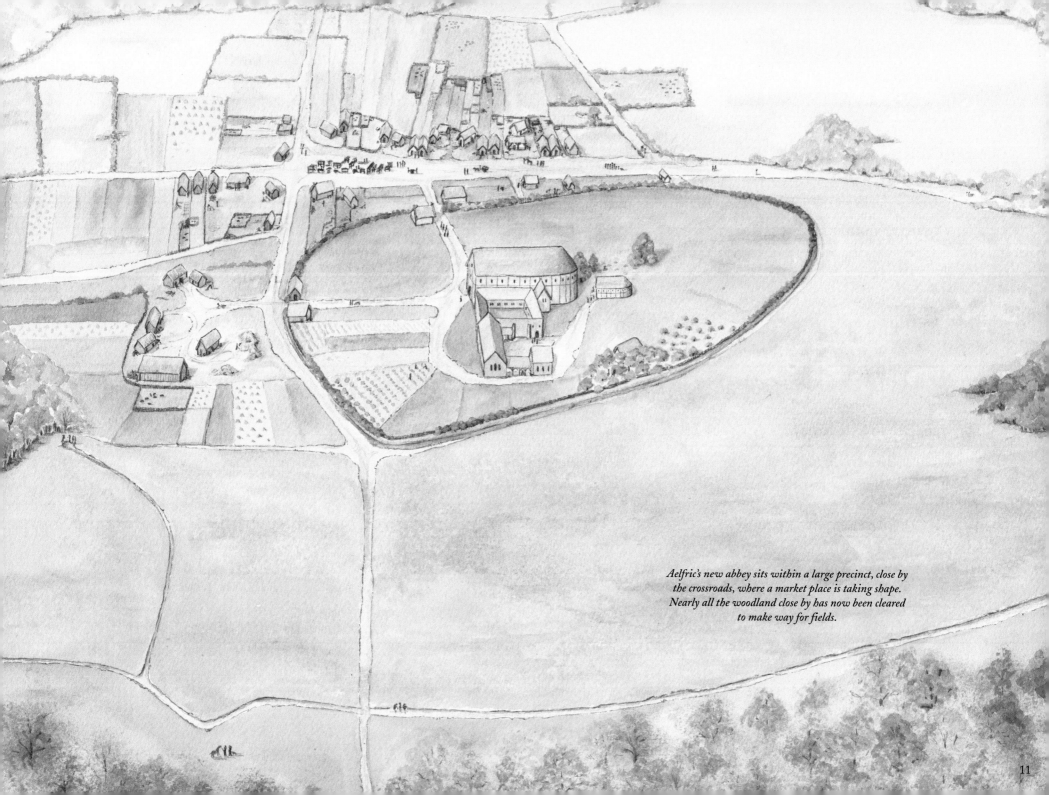

Aelfric's new abbey sits within a large precinct, close by the crossroads, where a market place is taking shape. Nearly all the woodland close by has now been cleared to make way for fields.

On the brink....

The Norman Conquest of 1066 caused widespread panic and disorder in the south of England. Later records talk of the monks of Eynsham fleeing the 'enemy', and the abbey being 'laid waste'. Was this true?

Soon after the Conquest, the old see of Dorchester was amalgamated with Caistor and Lincoln was made the new centre. Eynsham was now too far from the centre of church power to be at all important, and the new Bishop of Lincoln, Remegius, appointed by William the Conqueror, planned to transfer the monks of Eynsham and the abbey properties to Stow in Lincolnshire, and there make a new, larger monastery.

The process would take some years, so in the meantime, Eynsham was left with a 'caretaker' head, the monk Columbanus.

He and his few assistants were on the brink of leaving for Stow when Remegius died. His successor Robert Bloet, with the support of the King, decided to abandon the plan, and reinstate Eynsham as a fully fledged abbey. Maybe the position of Eynsham, near the King's new hunting lodge at Woodstock, made it seem more attractive.

The dig found no trace that the old abbey had been laid waste by violence, and instead found traces of a large kitchen - obviously intended to serve many people - built in the last decade of the 11th century. Very puzzling!

Above: The large hearth of the kitchen built at the end of the 11th century - the hole was made many years later.

What is a see? As kings and chieftains would divide up the land into their territories for political control, so the church leaders would divide the land for religious control. Each main area - or 'see' would have its own bishop, and his seat - or 'cathedra' would be in his main church. Later these churches became 'cathedrals'. The 'see' of Lincoln is shown on the map below.

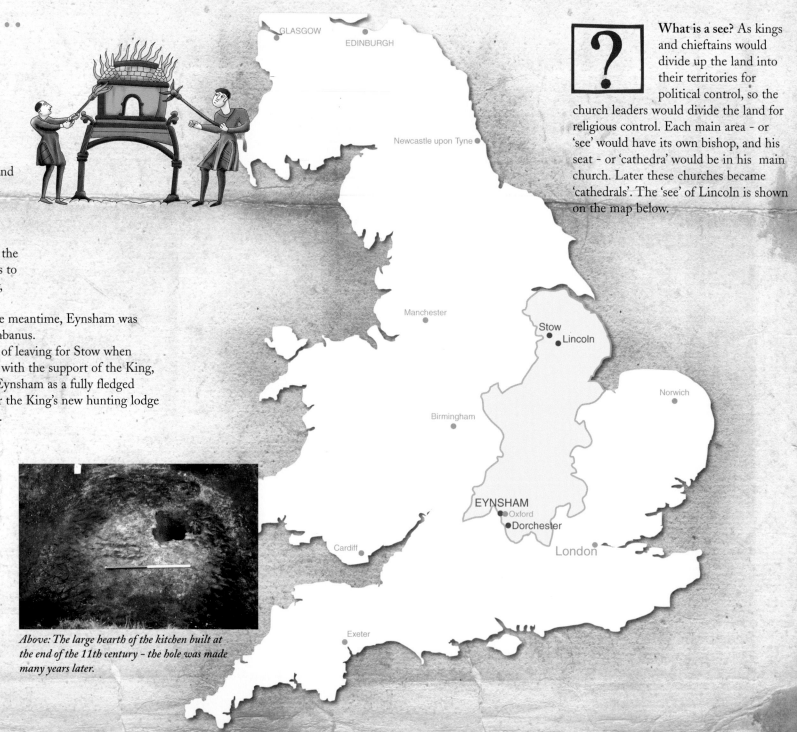

A SECOND FOUNDATION

NORMAN EYNSHAM

The process of refounding an abbey at Eynsham took time, and it was not until 1109 that Henry I signed the charter at Westminster, declaring:

> "In the name of the holy and undivided Trinity, Father Son and Holy Spirit.
> I, HENRY, king of England, with the assent and counsel of my bishops and barons, have determined to re-establish and confirm Eynsham abbey.....which right until now has lain deserted, with its affairs in disarray......And this shall be for the salvation of the souls of my father and mother and of my brother William, and for my own salvation, and that of my wife and children. I grant also to the same church all that my faithful people have given to it or will in future give to it, for the salvation of their souls."

The caretaker abbot, Columbanus, oversaw the beginning of the rebuilding. Whatever was left of the old abbey was cleared and a completely new church and all the other buildings necessary for a self-sufficient abbey were built. Such work took time, and work began with the east end of the church, where the holy services would be held. Next would come the cloister and chapter house, refectory, kitchen and dormitory.

? **Why so much fuss about the old abbey?** The advisors of King Henry I were well aware of the unease in the country, left over from William's conquest, and the appointment of Norman bishops. They had to make it look as though the old Saxon church organisation had broken down. By describing the old Saxon abbey as run down, deserted or even destroyed, the refoundation of Eynsham Abbey would bring great credit upon King Henry, and reassure doubters that the future of the Christian religion in the country was in good hands.

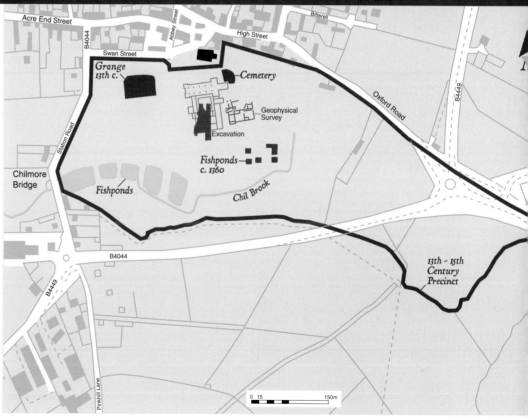

Above: The layout of the refounded abbey and its precinct in relation to the modern village.

13

In the service of God

An abbey was a place where monks could devote their lives to worship away from the temptations of the outside world. The church and the cloister were the heart of that world, and were arranged according to strict rules. The cloister was a square courtyard, surrounded by a covered passage, where monks could work at desks, exercise, and talk. In the open square was the lavatorium - a fountain and washing place. On the east side of the cloister was the chapter house where the business of the abbey was conducted. Further south was the dormitory, where the monks slept. On the west side were guest lodgings and the abbot's own house. On the south side was the communal eating hall - the refectory, and attached to this was the kitchen.

The monks' behaviour was as closely regulated as the buildings. Some of the rules were the same for all abbeys, some were specially written for the particular house. They would often be bound together as a Customary - a handbook for monks.

The dig uncovered part of the cloister and the remains of a large circular fountain. Part of the original pavement was still in place. Some fragments of painted plaster were found, indicating that the cloister walls were decorated.

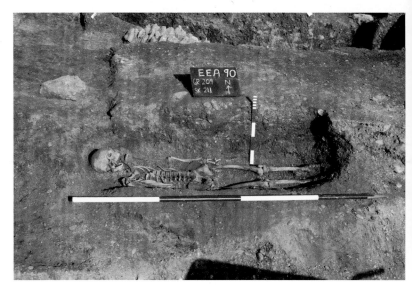

One of the burials found under the cloister.

Six burials were uncovered under the cloister floor. Abbots and senior monks were usually buried in the chapter house or in the cemetery to the east of the church. Five of the burials found were of young men, probably junior monks.

Part of the cloister pavement.

The Customary
The Eynsham Customary was written by Brother John of Wood Eaton. Churches were always cold and damp, and monks often had colds and coughs, so one instruction was:

HOW TO BEHAVE WHEN EXPELLING PHLEGM....

"When he has expelled phlegm, whether from his nose or his chest, he should behave with care and consideration, casting it in front or to one side or behind his back, and (so far as necessary) treading on what he casts. Otherwise he may make more sensitive spirits feel sick, or he may soil the garments of the brethren who are bowed in prayer. This is the decent way to behave, not only in church, but in the community."

OVERLEAF:
The cloister as it may have looked in the 13th century.

14

Feeding the abbey

If the cloister was the centre of the monks' spiritual life, then the kitchen was the heart of their practical life. It was a large building, with fireplaces in the corners, and ovens and open hearths in the centre. The smoke went out through chimneys or a central hole in the roof. Because of the danger of fire, the roof was very high, and because of the heat, there were just canvas screens over the windows, no glass.

A lot of the monks' food would be vegetables and beans, grown on the abbey farm, and made more tasty with herbs from the kitchen garden and spices brought by the cellarer who was in charge of the abbey's food supply.

Often abbey kitchen floors would be made of stone slabs, which would be brushed clean daily. At Eynsham, the floor was just mortar. As the ash from the fires built up, it was sealed with a fresh patch of mortar to keep down the dust. The process was repeated again and again, so that the floor level rose by 70 cm over 300 years!

This was great news for the bone experts on the dig, because thousands of small animal and fish bones were preserved in the layers. These told us that a staple part of the monks diet was herring, which would have been brought from the east coast of England packed in barrels of preserving salt. The monks would only be allowed meat - like beef or mutton - on feast days, unless they were sick, when they were fed from the infirmary (hospital) kitchen on the far side of the abbey grounds.

 The dig also found the bones of more exotic animals like deer, geese, swans and even spoonbill. These would usually be served for important guests of the abbot.

Monks would not normally drink water - it was not clean. Their usual drink was beer, made by the abbey's own brewhouse. The daily beer allowance was generous - sometimes over-generous, especially for senior monks and abbots. In 1284, it was found that retired abbot John had

 The dig found that the new kitchen for the refounded abbey was very unusual, separate from the refectory, with big rounded fireplaces in the corners. For some reason this building was never finished, and a new one - more typical in shape - was built in its place.

Above: The alternate layers of mortar and ash in the medieval kitchen, showing in the side of the trench.

mistakenly been given an allowance of eight gallons (36 litres) per day! This was too much, and it was reduced to just four gallons per day, and half that would have to go to his companion monk!

The Benedictine diet

Two meals a day were allowed with two dishes of cooked food at each meal. A pound of bread (half a kilogramme) per day was permitted. The flesh of four-footed animals was prohibited for all monks except for the sick and the weak.

Above: The cellar where the food was stored.

Herring with sauce vert (green sauce)

"Take percely, myntes, peletre a foil or if oj of cost marye, a cloue of garleke. And take faire brede, and stepe it with vynegre and piper, and salt; and grynde all this to-gedre, and tempre it up with wynegre, or with eisel, and serue it forth."

Recipe for sauce vert dated 1439

The ordinary monk's diet was restricted by the Benedictine rule, so that a large part of their diet would have been salted or pickled fish, or - in the case of cod - dried fish known as 'stockfish'. However, exceptions were made for the abbot and his guests at Eynsham, and the abbey's well-stocked fishponds would have given them a reliable source of fresh fish, and while not commonly eaten today, pike would have featured quite often on the abbot's menu. The recipe here is for a cold sauce used to dress poached or broiled fish and was a popular medieval dish.

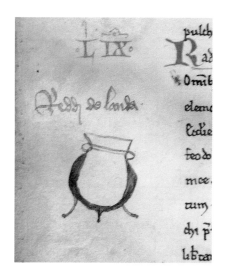

Above: A doodle of a cooking pot in the margins of the Eynsham Cartulary.

Ingredients

the leaves of 10-11 sprigs parsley, mint and other fresh herbs
1 clove of garlic
2 oz (50g) fine 'white' breadcrumbs
2 tbls (30 ml) cider vinegar
large pinch salt
ground black pepper
wine vinegar and /or water as is needed

Chop the herbs finely. Crush and squeeze the fresh garlic juice over the herbs.
Sprinkle the breadcrumbs with the cider vinegar and leave for 10 minutes. Add to the herbs with the salt and pepper.
Pound in a mortar until well blended.
Then add enough white wine vinegar or water (or a mixture of both) to give a consistency rather like thickened bread sauce.
Serve with broiled or poached herring.

WATER

Water was symbolically important to cleanse the monks of the dirt or sin of the real world. In a practical sense it was vital in a community like this, in the preparation and cooking of food, and the provision of safe and clean sanitation.

This relatively high level of cleanliness meant that in times of plague monasteries were often the safest places to live. During the middle years of the 14th century when the Black Death raged across Britain, fatalities in most monasteries were remarkably low in contrast to the rest of the population - a fact that was seen as evidence of the miraculous at the time.

Later abbeys were often built over fast-flowing streams to provide a good supply of running water. Earlier abbeys like Eynsham relied first on wells and local springs. One spring existed at the western end of what is now Conduit Lane, which is how it got its name. Where the spring came out of the ground a well-house was built, and the water was directed down Mill Street, across the Market Square, past (or possibly under) the church and into the cloister.

There it was directed to the fountain (lavatorium), and from there through the refectory to the kitchen. The water was carried in lead pipes wrapped in soft clay and buried in the ground.

The dig found the trenches where the pipes had been laid, and the soft clay, but almost all of the lead pipe had been removed when the abbey was demolished. Only one piece of pipe remained, which would have fed a tap in the kitchen.

Above:
This medieval well house in North Yorkshire shows how the Eynsham well house may have looked, with the spring head protected by a stone chamber, and the water lead away in a stone channel. Photograph by Patrick Greene.

Above:
A length of lead pipe, part of the water system found during the excavation.

& WASTE

Carefully constructed drains were built to carry the waste water away from the buildings. Getting rid of toilet waste was more difficult. Some abbeys built their toilets over streams, which would flush away the waste easily. With no convenient stream, at Eynsham they built large stone-lined latrine pits. Every so often these would have to be emptied - by hand!

This at least was a job the monks would have employed someone else to do for them, professional latrine pit emptiers called 'gongfermors'. They emptied cesspits and latrines using a bucket and a long handled wooden spade.

At least one member of this medieval profession met his end in the line of duty, as we know in 1326 Richard the Raker, a London gongfermor fell through some rotten boards and into the pit below and and was said by witnesses to have "Drowned Monstrously in the excrement".

By the 12th century when the abbey was thriving, other rubbish, like waste food from the kitchen or broken pottery, was taken well away from the buildings and either buried in pits or spread on the fields. Very few rubbish pits of this time were found in the dig

Some of the drains and cesspit under excavation.

A face from the past - could this be an ancestor of someone in the village today?

The rude tile!

One of the drains uncovered was lined with roof tiles. One of them had a face marked on one side - the face shows a man with shoulder length hair, and a long drooping nose. Most likely it was made by a bored tile maker, poking fun at his foreman!

It is clearly not meant to be flattering, but it is the nearest we can get to a snapshot of a real person of the time - possibly even an ancestor of someone living in the village today!

THE EXPANSION

MEDIEVAL EYNSHAM

As the abbey grew in size and wealth, the old precinct limits became constricting. In the early 13th century the ambitious Abbot Adam set out to rectify matters by buying up land to the south and east of the abbey, and in doing so more than doubled the size of the precinct. Enlarging the precinct meant closing part of what is now Abbey Street, and building a new road (now Station Road) along the new western boundary.

Fishponds

Many abbeys were now building their own fishponds, to supply the abbots and his guests with fresh pike and other fish. In 1217 Adam built a set of large fishponds, (above) fed by the Chil Brook. One of the properties he bought was a moated house belonging to Harvey, son of Peter. The moat and platform are still visible just south of fishponds, although no building remains survive.

> "...There is on the western side of the abbey a large court, in which there are situated granges and other buildings for oxen, cows and sheep, and for receiving other stock live and dead..."

Extract from a survey of the farm in 1360.

The story of...Abbot Adam

One abbot stands head-and shoulders above the rest for ambition, achievement and sheer nerve, Adam was born in Oxford and became a monk at Eynsham, rising through the ranks to become Prior, and eventually Abbot. In his youth he wrote two famous books - the Life of St Hugh - the story of a French monk who eventually became Bishop of Lincoln, and the Vision of the Monk of Eynsham - an account of a mystic experience undergone by Adam's brother Edmund.

Once he became Abbot, Adam set about a major expansion of the abbey precinct, buying up land and property to the west, redirecting the roads and building the large flight of fishponds which can still be seen today. He went further, encouraged by the sight of the thriving monasteries in Oxford involving themselves in property speculation. In 1215 he laid out an entire new borough along both sides of what is now Newlands. The intention was to keep the rents for the new properties low, to encourage people to move there from high-rent Oxford, and so to revive Eynsham's flagging markets. His plan failed and he ran up such large debts (owing '£150 to David the Jew') that the abbey was nearly bankrupted, and Adam was deposed.

The 13th century abbey dominates the village, which is spreading out from the market place. Abbey Street is closed off, and development of Newlands has begun at the north end of the village.

Eynsham's wealth

How wealthy was the abbey? In 1390 the total income was £772 12s 10½d, of which £348 came from rents. The rest came from the sale of wool or livestock. In 1406 the total income had risen to £812 10s 8½d.

An abbey cost a great deal to maintain. Like others, Eynsham Abbey owned land, manors and churches given by the king or the nobility. Most of these were in north and west Oxfordshire - places like Yarnton, Deddington, Milton -Under-Wychwood, but some were much further afield, like Histon in Cambridgeshire. Single properties in Eynsham were often bequeathed to the abbey, which then would rent them out to tenants. The rents were carefully recorded, and often took the form of certain items, or days of service on the abbey farm, rather than money.

The 'land de Colestona' was granted by Abbot Godfrey for the sum of '10s per year and an iron pot paid each year at Easter'. As another example John 'the doorkeeper' was required to pay a pound of cumin to the Abbot at Michaelmas every year instead of the annual rent of fourpence.

The markets granted to the abbey by King Henry II and King Stephen at first drew lots of people and trade to the village, but gradually Eynsham was overtaken by Oxford and Witney, so by the 14th century, only one landholder was recorded as the son of a merchant (John the son of Stephen the merchant). The village came to rely almost totally upon the abbey.

The Abbot's expenses for one year - 1406

Apart from food, the monks had a small allowance to buy clothes. The abbot would usually have a better diet, and much more money to buy personal items, such as these:

....for one pair of boots 2s 6d; for another pair of boots 2s 6d; item, in occasional repair of boots 16d; and for the making and repairing of boots at other times 16d; for one pair of hose 14d; for 3 caps 2s; for gloves 8d; for 1 cowl 14s 6d; for one pair of straylis 9s 6d; for 1 ounce of black silk 12d; for 1 pair of spurs 10d; for 1 silk belt studded with gilded silver 12s 3d; item, given to master John Merston for his work in connection with abbot's illness 13s 4d; and to master John Wyttenam for the same reason 13s 4d; for medicines and spices bought at the time of the abbot's illness 5s; for various medicines made for the lord abbot by master John Merston at various times and master John Wyttenam 29s 3d, as is shown in detail in the cellarer's book.

Sum: 110s 6d

A medieval hotel

Like many abbeys, Eynsham had to combine a private holy world for its monks, and guest quarters for all manner of visitors and travellers, from every part of society. Many were pilgrims, coming to see the relic of St Andrew, often on the way from another shrine - at Canterbury, for instance. They would be housed in the almonry, a building thought to have stood at the top of what is now Station Road. Visiting priests or monks would stay in guest lodgings closer to the heart of the abbey. The most upheaval was caused by the occasional visits of the King himself. As the Royal hunting lodge was close by at Woodstock, he would often bring a retinue of courtiers and officials with him. This could stretch the abbey's resources to the limit. The accounts of 1390 record repairs being made to the bakehouse prior to the visit of King Richard II, and the sum of 16s 7d being spent on bread "bought on occasion for the abbot, convent and guests; it was so much because the monastery's oven was taken over by the lord king's bakers…".

Among the finds from the dig was a lead plaque - a pilgrim badge, showing St Thomas of Canterbury on a donkey or ass.

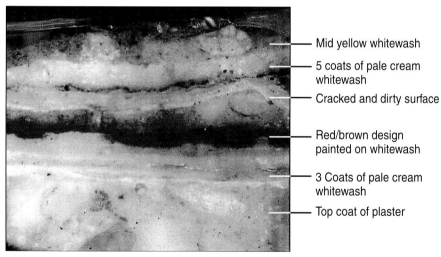

- Mid yellow whitewash
- 5 coats of pale cream whitewash
- Cracked and dirty surface
- Red/brown design painted on whitewash
- 3 Coats of pale cream whitewash
- Top coat of plaster

Medieval DIY! - A close-up photograph of the layers of paint and whitewash on a fragment of wall plaster from the guest hall.

 The dig found part of a guest hall with its own toilet block. The decoration inside was well maintained - small pieces of wall plaster showed that the walls had been regularly redecorated.

Pilgrim badges

Pilgrims were a common sight in abbey towns like Eynsham. They would tour the country, visiting the relics of Saints and other holy places. They felt that the more places they visited, the more they made sure they would go to heaven. To show others that they had visited a shrine, they would buy a badge - very like the badges we buy today to show we have been to a certain holiday resort! Eynsham had its own shrine, containing a relic of St Andrew, and the abbey would have sold images of St Andrew to visiting pilgrims.

THE FINAL DAYS

TUDOR EYNSHAM

Henry VIII, wanting to free both himself and England from the ties to Rome and the Catholic Church, declared himself head of the new Anglican Church, and felt free to close all the hundreds of monasteries and abbeys in the country, confiscating their huge wealth. To make it appear justified, Henry's right-hand man, Cardinal Wolsey, had officials inspect all religious houses, and encouraged them to find fault and depict the monks as lazy immoral scroungers. Inspector Tregonwell in 1535:

> "At Eynsham I found a raw sort of religious persons and all sort of offences among them......The abbot is chaste in his living, looks well to the reparation of the house: but he is negligent in overseeing his brethren, which he excuses by his daily infirmity."

The abbey was surrendered to the King on December 4th 1538, and the monks were pensioned off. Within a few weeks most of the buildings - especially the church - would have been made unusable by stripping the lead and timber from the roofs and removing the windows. The site became the property of the Edward Stanley, the Earl of Derby, who occasionally lived there - probably in the abbot's lodgings which would have been spared the ransacking.

Some of the fittings from the church itself ended up in the rubbish on the site, including hundreds of fragments of window glass. Among these were three pieces showing the faces of Saint Andrew, the Virgin Mary, and Christ.

The dig found evidence that the latrine pits had been used as rubbish skips for all the useless material from the rest of the site, like door locks, furniture fittings, and even specimen jars (urinals)! Of the buildings excavated, only the kitchen continued in use, and it produced pieces of fine Venetian glassware that must have been used by the Stanley family.

*Left:
The latrine pits under excavation.*

The last 10 monks -
and their pensions

(As the average farm labourer's wage was around £5 per year, you can see that the pension for the ordinary monk was not exactly generous!)

1. Anthony Dunstone (Abbot) - £133/6/8d - he became Bishop of Llandaff
2. Edmund Raynsford (Prior) - £10/0/0d
3. George Brodehurst - £6/13/4d
4. Thomas Mill - £5/6/8d
5. Thomas Phillips - £5/6/8d
6. Thomas Knollis - £5/6/8d
7. Robert Ford - £5/6/8d
8. John Coxeter - £5/6/8d
9. William Buck - £5/6/8d
10. John Hedges - £5/6/8d

One of the fragments of window glass.

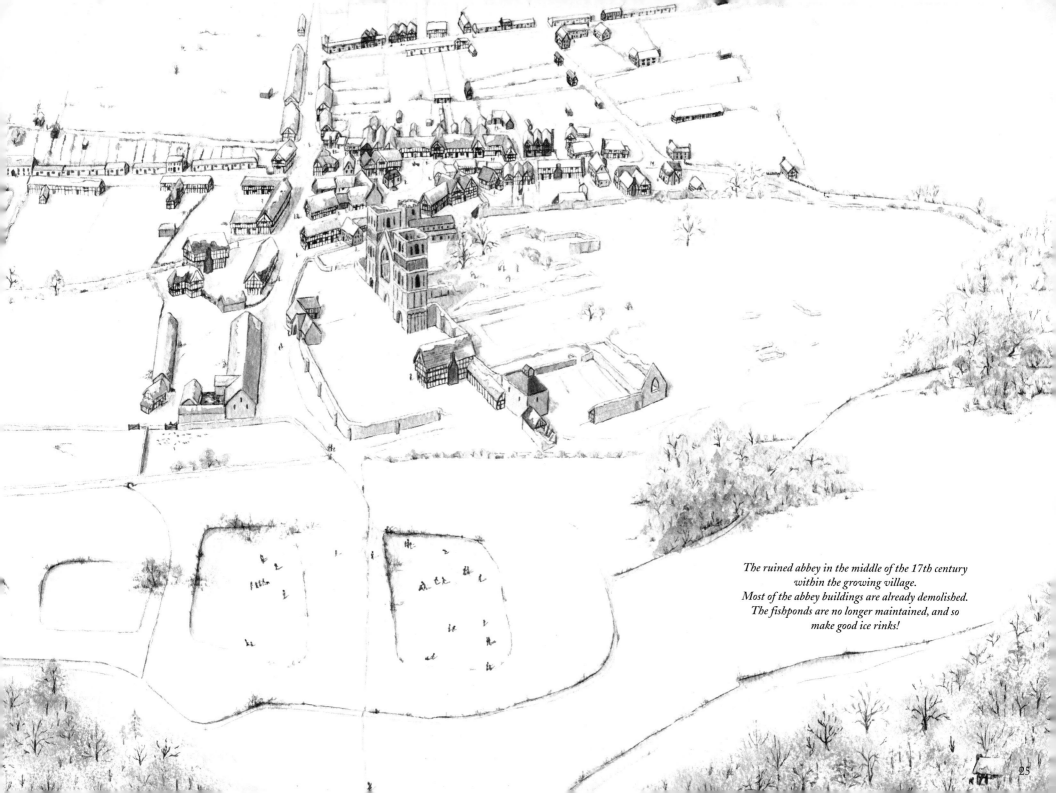

The ruined abbey in the middle of the 17th century within the growing village. Most of the abbey buildings are already demolished. The fishponds are no longer maintained, and so make good ice rinks!

Into the mists of legend

For over 100 years the derelict abbey stood, and much of the grounds became overgrown woodland. The Stanley family were strong Catholics and supported the recusants, those who refused to give up their faith. One of the Stanleys' staff was Thomas Barncote, who in 1630 was excommunicated for assisting in the burial, at night-time, of an excommunicant, "in a close called the park on the backsyde of Eynsham Abbey". The same man was the uncle of Anthony Wood, who in 1657 came to visit, and drew a rough sketch of the ruined church. Within a few months of his visit the abbey site was bought by a cloth manufacturer, Thomas Jordan, who swiftly demolished the entire abbey complex, and sold off the stone.

In the following centuries, travellers would be told fabulous stories of what had been there - of "a world of painted glass". One traveller - Thomas Hearne - was told in 1706 by some aged villagers that there had been 52 fishponds belonging to the abbey (one for every week of the year)! Indeed, so little was remembered, that some thought it had been the site of a castle. Successive copies were made of Anthony Wood's sketch, but the results became more and more unrealistic and confusing.

Who were the recusants?

By the late 16th century, England was officially a Protestant country. Catholics were tolerated, but they had to attend Protestant church services. If they refused, they could be fined, publicly shamed and eventually excommunicated, which meant they could not be buried in consecrated ground. For God-fearing people, this meant everlasting damnation in the afterlife. People who stood fast to their faith - and there were many in Oxfordshire - were called recusants.

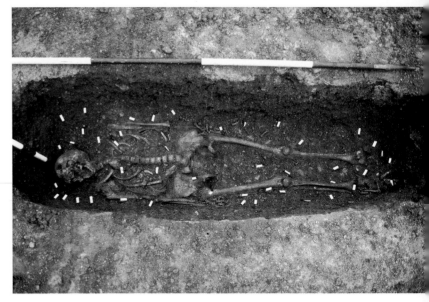

One of the recusant burials - the white tags mark the position of coffin nails.

The dig found three burials in the refectory, put there after the abbey was abandoned by the monks, but before the final demolition. This one - of a middle aged man - had many broken bones. Were these three recusants? And if so, had this man suffered a terrible beating before his death?

The dig found a thick layer of mortar from the final demolition of the abbey. It seems that the stones were brought to the area of the cloister - where they were cleaned and sorted, and then carted off to make houses in the village and elsewhere. Many of the old cottages of the village have pieces of carved stone from the abbey within their walls.

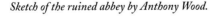

Sketch of the ruined abbey by Anthony Wood.

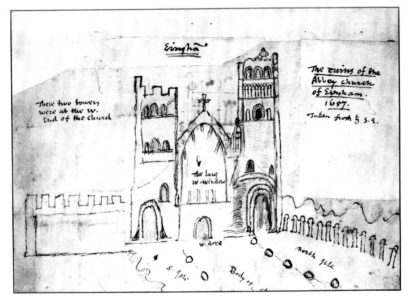

Anthony Wood 1632 -1695

He lived all his life in Merton Street, Oxford, becoming famous as an antiquarian - a historian - and got into trouble by writing about the corruption in the University.

Anthony Wood.

..... And at last into daylight

The building of extensions to the graveyards of St Peter's and St Leonard's finally gave the archaeologists a chance to dig in 1989. Over two years, the team dug through over three thousand years of Eynsham's past, recovering a mountain of finds and an enormous amount of information.

It took ten years and a huge team of experts to analyse all the material, and put together the archaeological story. Like a giant jigsaw, piece by piece the evidence was fitted together to show how the site evolved. Then the archaeology and the results from the surveys were compared to the documentary history to see how they matched.

This story does not claim to be the final word on Eynsham Abbey - the area excavated is tiny compared to the whole precinct, and much more lies buried and protected for future generations to investigate - but at least a door to Eynsham's glorious past has been partly opened, and it shows that - almost a thousand years after its foundation, and five hundred since its destruction, the abbey still has a strong influence on the village.

The dig in progress in 1990.

Examining some of the environmental evidence.

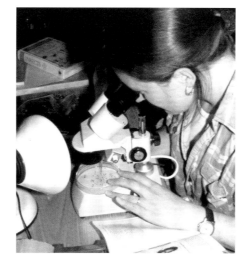

N

Bronze Age		Early Medieval
Saxon		Medieval
Late Saxon		Post-Dissolution

0   5   10   15m

Plan of the whole dig, showing the different phases of activity.

Eynsham, otherwise known as…

The name of the village has been spelled many different ways through the ages. Note that the modern spelling first occurred in the 14th century.

Egones ham (10th century)
Igeneshamme
Iogneshomme
Egenes homme
Eghenesham
Eogneshame
Eigenesham
Egenesham
Evenesham
Eglesham
Egglesam
Egnesham (11th century)
Einselsam
Eygnesham
Eignesham
Eisnesham
Einesham
Enesham
Heynesham
Heinesham
Aynesham
Ainesham
Enysham
Eylnesham
Einegham
Eynesham
Egnsham
Eynsham (1390)
Eynysham
Enesham
Eneysham
Enysham
Enisham
Enysam
Enensham
Enensam
Enseham
Egnosham
Evinsham
Evensham
Einsham
Ensham (18th century)

500 years of abbots

Not all of the abbots of Eynsham Abbey are known to us. These 30, the pious, the notorious, the good and the bad, all played their part in the story of the abbey.

1. Aelfric - 1005-1010 First and most famous abbot
2. Columbanus - ? known to be alive in 1086 and 1094
The 'caretaker' head of Eynsham during the years before the refoundation in 1109
3. Walter - ? known to be alive in 1129
Probably abbot when the abbey was refounded in 1109
4. Walter - ? - 1150?
The abbey acquired a hermitage in Bloxham forest
5. William - ?1150-1152
Witnessed a deed relating to Godstow nunnery
6. Godfrey - 1152-96
He was lazy and fond of amusements 'ludicra et inania' Gave the best abbey offices to his four nephews
7. Robert - 1197-1208
Began a (probably false) legal claim to gain possession of Yarnton
8. Adam - 1213-28
9. Nicholas - 1228-39
Previously prior of Frieston, Lincolnshire. Lived on at the abbey after his resignation
10. John de Douor 1239-41
In his time the relic of the arm of St Andrew was brought to Eynsham, and was claimed to cause many miracles.
11. Gilbert of Gloucester (1241-64)
Originally the cellarer at the abbey
12. Alexander of Brackley (1264-8)
13. John of Oxford (1268-81)
Appointed directly by the Bishop, rather than by an election of the monks of the abbey
14. Thomas of Wells (1281-1307)
In 1296 a huge riot left Oxford students dead and injured in Eynsham.
15. Adam of Lambourne (1307- 16)
16. John de Cheltenham (1317-30)
 Resigned through ill-health
17. John de Broughton (1330-38)
18. Nicholas de Upton (1338-44 and 1344-51)
19. William Staunford (1344)
20. Galfridus de Lambourn (1351-88)
21. Thomas Bradingstock (1388-1413)
22. James of Ramsden (1414-31)
23. Thomas Oxinford (1432 and 1434)
Not a credit to the abbey - pawned the abbey jewels to fund his loose living - found guilty by the Bishop of gross immorality
24. John Quenington (1441-57)
Cleaned up the abbey, which at this time contained 14 brothers
25. Robert Faryndone (1457-69)
26. William Walwayn (1469-?)
An outsider - there was not a monk at Eynsham sufficiently learned or capable to take the post.
27. Miles Salley (? - 1516)
Bishop of Llandaff- did not reside at Eynsham
28. Thomas Chaundler (1516-19)
29. Henry Riding (1519-30)
30. Anthony Dunstone (alias Anthony Kitchen) (1530-39)